Usborne First Experiences
Going on a Plane

Anne Civardi

Illustrated by Stephen Cartwright

Edited by Michelle Bates
Cover design by Neil Francis
Consultant: Jennifer Smith

There is a little yellow duck hiding on every page. Can you find it?

This is the Tripp family.

Tim Tripp

Mr. Tripp

Mrs. Tripp

Rosie Tripp

Lily Tripp

Rover

Tim and Rosie are helping Mr. and Mrs. Tripp to pack.
They are going on a plane tomorrow.

They set off for the airport.

Grandpa Tripp takes them in his car. Lily is staying behind with Granny and Rover, the dog.

Mr. Tripp unloads their bags.

One of them topples over. It is Rosie's. She collects her
things. "Sorry," says Mr. Tripp.

The Tripps check in.

"Here are the tickets," Mrs. Tripp says to the lady at the check-in counter. Another lady weighs their luggage.

The Tripps go through a metal detector.

Their bags go through an x-ray machine to make sure they are not carrying anything dangerous.

They board the plane.

A flight attendant shows them to their seats. Mr. Tripp puts their bags into a locker above their heads.

They're ready for take-off.

"Fasten your seat belts," says the flight attendant. "I've buckled Hippo in," says Rosie.

The plane takes off.

The pilot starts up the engines of the big plane. The flight attendant tells the passengers the safety rules.

The pilot waits for his turn to take off. Then the plane speeds down the runway and zooms up into the air.

It's time to eat.

"Here's your lunch," the flight attendant says to Mrs. Tripp. Tim can't wait to start eating his meal.

The flight attendant speaks to the pilots.

She goes into the cockpit and asks the pilots if they would like to have something to eat, too.

The plane will land soon.

Mrs. Tripp and Rosie go to use the toilet. Back in their seats, they listen to music on earphones.

Tim looks out of the window. "We're coming down," he shouts. Soon the plane lands safely on the runway.

The Tripps get off the plane.

They walk down the stairs to the bus that will take them to the airport building. "Catch my hat!" cries Mrs. Tripp.

They go through passport control.

PASSPORT CONTROL

An officer checks their passports. "Look," Rosie says to Mr. Tripp, "he's putting a big stamp in yours."

They collect their luggage.

They wait at the baggage carousel until their bags arrive.
"Here are my things," Rosie says to a porter.

The Tripps leave the airport.

Mrs. Tripp gives the porter some money. "Taxi, taxi," shouts Mr. Tripp. And off the Tripps go to their hotel!

This edition published in 2005 by Usborne Publishing Ltd, Usborne House, 83-85 Saffron Hill, London EC1N 8RT, England.
Copyright © 2005, 1992 Usborne Publishing Ltd. www.usborne.com
First published in America in 2005. UE
The name Usborne and the devices ♀ ⊕ are Trade Marks of Usborne Publishing Ltd.